YESTERDAY MY PAIN

TODAY MY POEM

TOMORROW MY PRAISE

POETRY

DOREEN MAMPANI

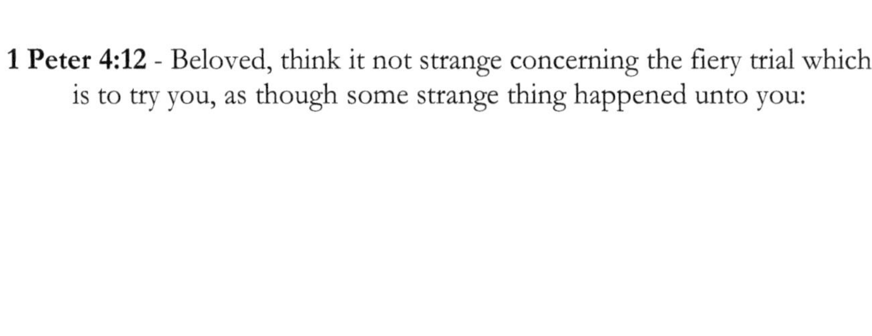

1 Peter 4:12 - Beloved, think it not strange concerning the fiery trial which is to try you, as though some strange thing happened unto you:

DEDICATION

I dedicate this book to God my Heavenly Father for His grace upon me and my child, L'amour. I also dedicate to all people who are battling against pain.

Contents

ACKNOWLEDGMENTS i

1. INTRODUCTION 3

2. ACCEPTING LORD JESUS CHRIST AS YOUR LORD AND SAVIOR...5

3. YESTERDAY MY PAIN TODAY MY POEM TOMORROW MY PRAISE..7

4. TRIBULATIONS ESCORTING SAINTS TO THE THRONE.......8

5. WORDS SPEAKS MORE THAN A SMILE 9

6. TEARS ON THE ROCK..11

7. THAT BRIGHT MORNING 13

8. SHALL I SING MY KING? 15

9. LORD JESUS CHRIST LORD OVER DEATH 16

10.   WHEN THE SLAVE SINGS A...18

11.   I'M JUST A ZIMBABWEAN REFUGEE 20

12.   I WISH TO GET EDUCATION..23

13.   A CRY OF A NIGERIAN MAN 25

14.   NO NEED TO WALK ALONE 28

15.   LOVE DEEPER THAN THE OCEANS.......................................30

16.   SHALL WE DANCE TODAY?..31

17. NO MULTIPLE CHOICE IN HEAVEN 32

18. BIBLE VERSES RELATED TO PAIN 34

19. CONCLUSION 36

ABOUT THE AUTHOR...38

BOOKS BY DOREEN MAMPANI 40

ACKNOWLEDGMENTS

I would like to acknowledge LORD Jesus Christ for His love and protection over me and L'amour.

1. INTRODUCTION

As long as we are in this world pain is unavoidable. The wise endure the pain every day. The tile *Yesterday My Pain Today My Poem Tomorrow My Praise* is about painful experiences that we have that God turns to our poems today then praise tomorrow. We look back and see situations that God saved us and realized that our pain becomes our poem. When we are victorious after overcoming the painful situation we praise God for these testimonies.

Pain if not attended to can lead to sorrow, shedding of tears that leads to depression and other diseases, ultimately death. It's important to pray about our pain.

James 5:13 "Is any among you afflicted? let him pray. Is any merry? let him sing psalms."

King David prayed when he was in pain. In Psalm 51 he repents of his sin while in pain.

Pain should be our teacher not our tormentor. When a woman is in child labor she travails in agony knowing that she will have a child to carry in her arms. Recently I saw a two month old baby. The mother had a very difficult pregnancy. I encouraged her from when she was 5 months pregnant until she gave birth. She was sick

"

during the pregnancy and God granted her the strength to carry the baby to full term. Today she forgot of all the sickness she had while pregnant and during child birth.

Our trials as Christians will come to an end when LORD Jesus Christ take our souls. We will shed no more tears in heaven. In this world we shed tears of sorrow.

When a sports person exercise there is muscle pain but he/she knows that his/her muscles are being strengthened. Maybe you are in pain of some  sort, I encourage you to tell heavenly Father about it. Our Savior is with us. So why not take time to pray.

2. ACCEPTING LORD JESUS CHRIST AS YOUR LORD AND SAVIOR

There is one thing I never forget when writing my books. I know it is not that I'm better that any writer out there, it is by God's grace that I write books. LORD Jesus Christ has become the Lover of my soul. If it was not of God's unconditional love to save a sinner like me I would have been long dead without even writing a single book. I don't claim to have achieved but daily carry my cross and follow LORD Jesus Christ.

Scriptures about Salvation

> ***Romans 10:9****"That if thou shalt confess with thy mouth the Lord Jesus, and shalt believe in thine heart that God hath raised him from the dead, thou shalt be saved."*

> ***Matthew 10:33*** *"But whosoever shall deny me before men, him will I also deny before my Father which is in heaven."*

> ***Acts 2:38*** *"Then Peter said unto them, Repent, and be baptized every one of you in the name of Jesus Christ for the remission of sins, and ye shall receive the gift of the Holy Ghost."*

If you have not accepted LORD Jesus Christ as your LORD and Savior I would like to encourage you to do so.

I would like to invite you to take that big step and accept LORD Jesus Christ in your life. Pray the following prayer:

Dear Heavenly Father God,

I come to you in the Name of Jesus Christ Your only begotten Son. I now realize that I have a choice to make concerning my life. I believe that Jesus died and shed His blood for my sins and rose from the dead giving me a way to fellowship with You and to live eternal life with You.

Knowing this, I choose to renounce my past and I accept the price Jesus Christ paid for me to be total and complete, because You said it was.

I want Jesus to be the owner of my life. I choose to live for Him from this moment on.

I believe right now that I am indeed Born Again. My spirit is a brand new creation and I stand before You, Heavenly Father, worthy because Jesus Christ justified me.

Thank You for loving me.
Amen

Find a Bible based church where LORD Jesus Christ is LORD and Savior.

You may not feel anything, it is by faith that we receive Salvation. Believe you are saved because you are.

Welcome to the family.

3.   YESTERDAY MY PAIN TODAY MY POEM TOMORROW MY PRAISE

24 February 2021

If souls shed tears mine would have filled tanks of water
Such pain too deep for my soul to endure
Early hours I lamented in deep pain
If tears could fill a bath mine would have

Rejection deep in my bones burned
God reminded me of Job
How his bones burned and burned
Job cursed not God our Creator

My pain has become my poem
My poem has become my praise
Yesterday tortured me with pain
Today turned the pain into poetry
So tomorrow turned my poem into praise

Tears of yesterday cannot blind my vision today
For poetry grew in my heart from pain
Focusing on poetry I find myself praising
Oh that God may fill my heart with melodies

Such praise in my heart deeply dwells
That my heart bubbles with the joy of the LORD
Indeed God has turned my mourning into dancing

4. TRIBULATIONS ESCORTING SAINTS TO THE THRONE

20 September 2021

Tears on the desert watering it
What are these, what are these?
Tears of the Saints falling on the ground

Loved ones martyred
last night

Blood on the dining
room floor
Blood of Saints crying
out to the Most High
God
Like the blood of Abel
that cried out
God the Creator heard
from His Throne

Gates that were closed
now open
Fields now ready for
harvest
Laborers from the

Almighty God
Soon very soon the Messiah will appear

Saints in chains bound for their faith
Jeremiah endured to the end
Isaiah on the table slaughtered
For their faith in the God of Israel

Tribulations too deep for human souls to bear
Just for our faith in Jesus Christ

5.   WORDS SPEAKS MORE THAN A SMILE

Sunday 18 October 2020

Shall I wait until tomorrow
Just to express my gratitude
Words speak more than a smile
For an African a smile means very little

Let my heart speak before my Maker
To express my gratitude from the depth of my being
Shall I wait until next week
Shall I tarry any longer to utter words

Why procrastinate until tomorrow to say words
For today is ours to live in
Tomorrow in the hands of God belongs
 So while we have today
Let us rejoice in the presence of our God

Let my heart be filled with the joy of the Lord
For the strength of God I daily need
To fill my heart my soul my spirit
That I may dance again before my God

Though trial come my way
Though tribulations rage like a storm
Great comfort in Your Word I find
Words Your Words alone gives me courage

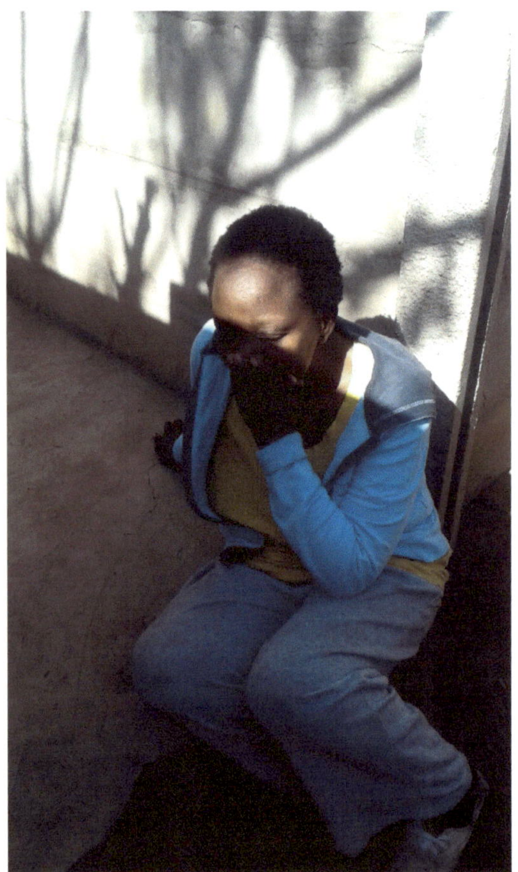

Me seating on the floor

6.   TEARS ON THE ROCK

20 September 2021

On his knees he cried out to his Maker
Salvation of souls his burden was
Little sleep daily he had
Just to be on his knees to intercede

So daily he lamented for souls
Lost souls, souls in chains
So the villagers walked
past the rock
To see tears on the rock

Like a sinner who cried
Only by grace we are
saved
So burdened was the man
With salvation of souls of
humanity

Little did the man daily
eat
Praying while he
ploughed his field
A great honour he
desired not
Just a laborer in the Master's vineyard

Tears on the rock were found
As though he could bath with it
Lost souls, lost souls so he cried out
Salvation of lost souls!

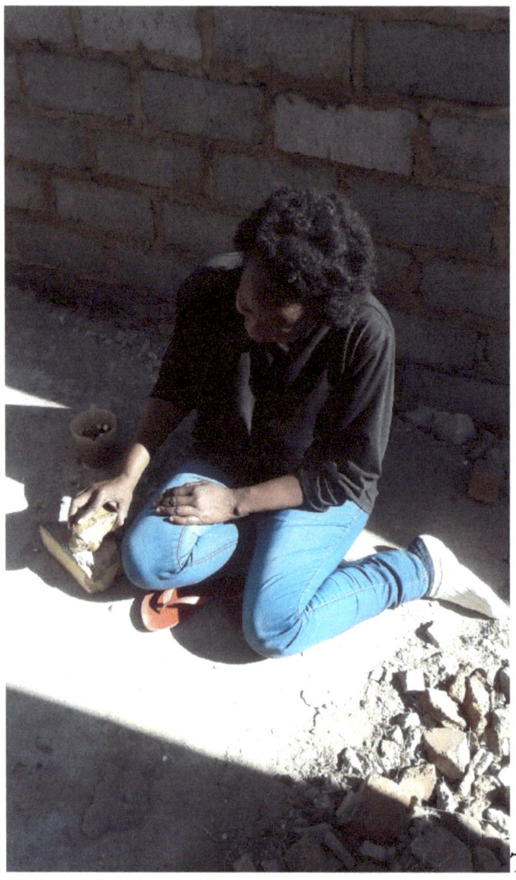

That's me crushing some nuts

7.   THAT BRIGHT MORNING

16 November 2020

Early, early morning the
birds sang
A beautiful song to their
Creator
Oh how I desire to be up
early
Just to say thank You my
Maker

The sun rising in the African
blue skies
A song of praise I sang that
morning
While I listened to the birds
that morning
So I started my own song

Alone I will never be
For Jesus Christ promised
never to leave me
Before sunrise I knelt down
Just to express my gratitude
to my Maker

A new song to my Maker I
sing

From the very depth of my being
Let every fiber of my being bow down
To adore to glorify my Heavenly Father

No need to shed tears of sorrow
But to stay on the narrow path

For wide is the gate to destruction
Help me, help me God to stay in faith

8.   SHALL I SING MY KING?

2 November 2020 (Night)

Give me a song a new song
Fill my heart with words
That I must sing early morning
To my Savior my Messiah

Fill my heart with a new song
Like You granted king David daily
Psalms to glorify his Creator
Shall I sing my King?

A song of gratitude a song of praise
Before my Savior I humbly bow
To bow my soul my entire being
To glorify God I AM

What is the right song to sing?
Shall I dance with the song of jubilee
Though I have many trials
Tribulations from every side
This I know my Savior my King
You will never leave me nor forsake me

9.   LORD JESUS CHRIST LORD OVER DEATH

Sunday: 7 March 2021

Many lords have come and gone
Great men whom the rich bowed their knees to
Men of great stature walked in power
Where the poor trembled in their presence

Death came took all the great men
If I mention names I'll fill a book
But while searching, searching and searching
The Only LORD Who overcame Death

Satan threw his worst on the Lamb of God
Crucifying LORD Jesus Christ on the cross
Death tried to rejoice but was cut short
For the sting of death lost its power on the Cross

Taking time to look in the graves of lords
Only one grave is permanently empty
His Name is the Name above all names

His Name makes death to flee

His Name heals all diseases
His Name causes Satan to flee
His Name brings life to the dead
The Name of Jesus Christ of Nazareth

We sang a song in church about LORD Jesus Christ being the Lord over death.

I walked in this area next to the grass and was almost attacked by a snake.

10. WHEN THE SLAVE SINGS A SONG

Sunday morning: 7 March 2021

If a slave cries all the time
A depressed slave he will become
More lashing on his back to receive
To die early to die prematurely

A depressed soul of a slave
Full of scars from all the beatings
So the slave woman heard a still small voice
Cry not My child cry no more
The Voice of her Maker spoke to her

 Bare feet for fifty
kilometers she
walked
To work for her
children
Little food she
could buy
Though she
earned a locust
She shared the
locust with her
neighbors

Oh Africa, Oh
Africa why cry to
your neighbor
Comfort from other continents you'll find not
Cry on your knees Africa

To your Redeemer
Tell not your calamities to your neighbor

Remember Africa king David looked to God
Day and night he cried out for help
Though a king he saw it not inferior
To ask help from the God

11. I'M JUST A ZIMBABWEAN REFUGEE

23 February 2021 - 12:08 PM

I walked for a thousand kilometers
Ran away from wild animals
I crossed the Limpopo River at night
By the grace of God the crocodiles didn't devour me

So hungry so thirsty yet I continued to walk

Just to get to South Africa for a 'piece job'
I met a madam to ask for a 'piece job'
To scrub her floors of a fifteen-bedroom house on my knees
With a hungry stomach I toiled

Given rotten food, expired milk
Oh how I ran to the toilet that night

Payday came for me to get my wages
Madam travelled to Cape Town for her holidays
Claiming she could

not pay me on time

So, I prayed on
my knees before
my Maker

God of heaven!
remember me a
Zimbabwean
refugee
My husband
died of Aids five
years ago
My mother died
of womb
fibroids
My father was
killed by robbers

Help me God!
Help me God
Just to find a
'piece job'
To feed my
children,
To feed my
mother- in-law,
Who daily takes
care of my
children

Though
Zimbabwe is the

last country on the world map
Before You my Maker we are important
Though we are the poorest in Africa
Amongst the rich in faith in You we are
I am a Zimbabwean Refugee

That's me on a farm

12.   I WISH TO GET EDUCATION

Mama said I can't go to school
'cause mama is too poor to pay my school fees
Pastor offered to pay for my school fees
But mama refused
saying Pastor is fake
I thought mama
loved me

I'm only fifteen years
supposed to be a
teenager
But a mother of
twins I am
Married to an old
man my grandpa's
age called a Blessor
Mama said I'm the
solution to fight
poverty in our family
My husband paid
lobolla with five
cattle
Mama sold the cattle to pay for my sibling's education

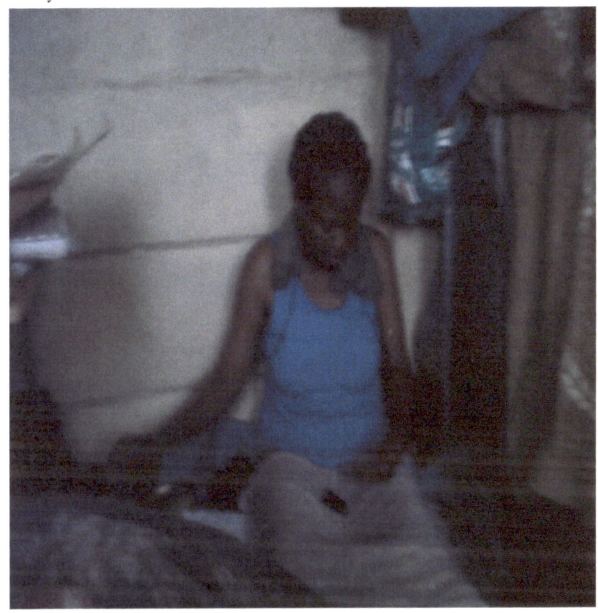

I cried of this injustice under the sun
Though I'm intelligent I can't go to school
Mama said it's our culture
The first-born sacrificed for her siblings
Who will bring me out of this calamity?
I am a child but forced to be a wife

Only God can help me now
To gain rights that mama violated
I write my story my book
To share with the world my injustice
Truly God loves a nobody like me

A picture of a "container" that I took

13.   A CRY OF A NIGERIAN MAN

Though my nationality is judged by those who lack knowledge
That many Nigerian men are drug dealers
Believe me when I tell you my brother
A God-fearing law-abiding Nigerian I am

Trust me my South African sister when I say
My marriage to you is not a marriage of convenience
Tomorrow I'll fly you to Nigeria
That you meet my mama in my native land
To assure you that my yes is yes and my no is no

Let me teach you my mother's tongue
While I diligently learn your language and your culture
This I say from the depth of my heart

You are the wife I've asked God for
Far be it from me that I lie before my Creator and before my elders

So proud I am to be a responsible Nigerian
Prejudice against me is due to lack of knowledge
A trustworthy man I am
Today I stand to represent not only Nigeria

But Africa as an

African man
Oh how I pray on my knees
That perception about Nigerian men be rectified in the world
For some suffered mob justice
For crimes they never committed

This pictures shows the brokenness of some refugees. When they cry out to God, He surely do answer and change their situations.

that's

me in the hot sun

14. NO NEED TO WALK ALONE

Loving the outcast the rejected of the world

8 October 2020 (Night)

Though it was dark at
night
No moon no stars
shining
No friend to say a
word of courage
A true friend in Jesus
Christ I found

Though I walked in the
dark
Like the valley of the
shadow of death itself
Deep in my heart I am
encouraged
For I know Jesus
Christ is with me

His promises are
always fulfilled
His Word is yeah and
Amen
So I realized that day
That never will I be
alone

Such love beyond
human understanding

Providing for the destitute in the world
No need to walk alone

With a grateful heart I come my Maker
Just to express my gratitude to You
No need to walk alone.

15. LOVE DEEPER THAN THE OCEANS

8 October 2020 (Night)

Even though I travelled in the world
To go to the four corners of the earth
To search for love to search for peace
Love like that of Jesus Christ
I will not find

Human love can fade away
Human love can grow cold
The love of God grows more and more
Love deeper than the oceans

Shall I dive in the oceans
To search for love that will satisfy
The heart of humanity all the time
Love deeper than the oceans

Love of the Creator of humanity
His love never running out
Love of God filling the hearts of people
Love deeper than the oceans

16.   SHALL WE DANCE TODAY?

8 October 2020

Big space before us is
Right music playing for us
No need to wait until tomorrow
Shall we dance today my love?

Never do lovers procrastinate
To dance when the music is on
Perhaps let us go to the garden
Let's take the music with

1 March 2021

Forbid her not to dance alone
Let her dance before her Creator
For David danced before His maker alone

The floor is calling out to the eunuch
To dance before the King of kings
Why forbid him when he desires
To worship I AM that I AM

17. NO MULTIPLE CHOICE IN HEAVEN

1 March 2021

If exams were written in heaven
Essays about the Ancient of Days would be asked
Questions on who LORD Jesus Christ is would be asked
Questions about the Holy Spirit would be asked

Diligent preparation from all Saints is vital
Searching the Ancient Words day and night
Asking the Helper for assistance night-through
No multiple choice in Heaven

A child of God has no room for doubt
Guess-work is strictly forbidden
In the exam room of heaven
LORD Jesus Christ the owner of exams
Given His all on the Cross

Say not the Bible is a big Book
Too complicated for the human mind
Take it one page at a time
Asking the God to help you
With understanding of the Ancient Words

So prepare while here under the sun
Though tribulations come stay in faith
When storms of life rage lean on Him
When trials come run to Jesus Christ

That's me preparing a table

18.　BIBLE VERSES RELATED TO PAIN

Revelation 21:4 – And God shall wipe away all tears from their eyes; and there shall be no more death, neither sorrow, nor crying, neither shall there be any more pain: for the former things are passed away.

Romans 8:18 - For I reckon that the sufferings of this present time are not worthy to be compared with the glory which shall be revealed in us.

1 Peter 4:12-19 - Beloved, think it not strange concerning the fiery trial which is to try you, as though some strange thing happened unto you:

Psalms 41:3 - The LORD will strengthen him upon the bed of languishing: thou wilt make all his bed in his sickness.

Job 30:17 - My bones are pierced in me in the night season: and my sinews take no rest.

1 Peter 4:12-13 - Beloved, think it not strange concerning the fiery trial which is to try you, as though some strange thing happened unto you:

1 Peter 4:19 - Wherefore let them that suffer according to the will of God commit the keeping of their souls to him in well doing, as unto a faithful Creator.

Jeremiah 15:18 - Why is my pain perpetual, and my wound incurable, which refuseth to be healed? wilt thou be altogether unto me as a liar, and as waters that fail?

Philippians 4:13 - I can do all things through Christ which strengtheneth me.

Job 14:22 - But his flesh upon him shall have pain, and his soul within him shall mourn.

1 Corinthians 6:19-20 - What? know ye not that your body is the temple of the Holy Ghost which is in you, which ye have of God, and ye are not your own?

Psalms 25:1-22 - (A Psalm of David.) Unto thee, O LORD, do I lift up my soul.

Jeremiah 29:11 - For I know the thoughts that I think toward you, saith the LORD, thoughts of peace, and not of evil, to give you an expected end.

Revelation 21:6-7 - And he said unto me, It is done. I am Alpha and Omega, the beginning and the end. I will give unto him that is athirst of the fountain of the water of life freely

Proverbs 20:30 - The blueness of a wound cleanseth away evil: so do stripes the inward parts of the belly.

Job 33:19 - He is chastened also with pain upon his bed, and the multitude of his bones with strong pain

19.   CONCLUSION

We have to daily choose to make "the joy of the LORD our strength". We have to choose to bear the fruit of the Holy Spirit according to Galatians 5.

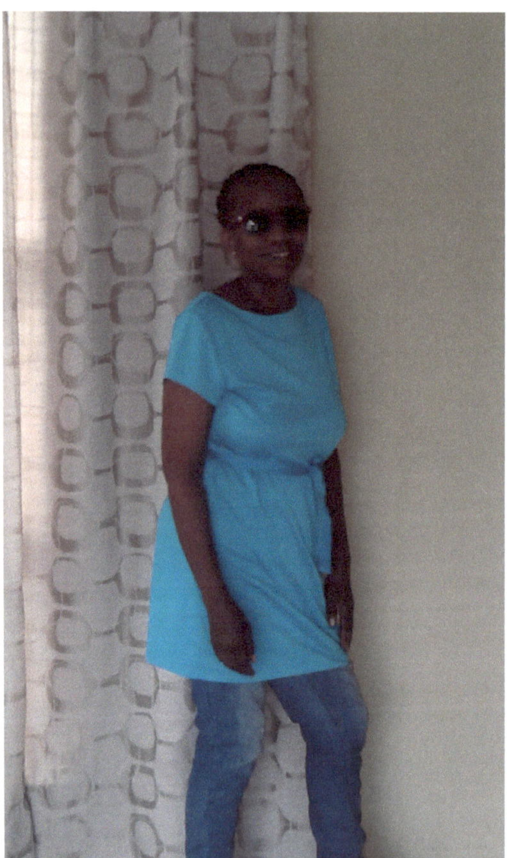

"We walk by faith and not by sight". If we depend on what we see we cannot have peace because of what happens in our lives, our homes, our neighborhood, our communities, cities, villages, country, continent and the world.

Every trial has an end, whether a good one of bad one. Pain cannot be there forever. "What the enemy meant for evil God will work it out for our good". My God turn your pain into a poem which will lead to praising God.

To endure until the end we need to lean on God and not on our own understanding. Our desire is to spend eternity with our Creator, the God of Israel.

I wrote these poems to express my own pain that God turned into poems then praises to God. We don't have to wait for our current pains to turn into poems but praise God for the blessings He has blessed us with all these years. To be alive and well is enough for us to thank God.

BIBLIOGRAPHY

Scriptures taken from the King James Bible

ABOUT THE AUTHOR

Doreen Mampani is a Christian author from the Republic of South Africa. She writes Christian non-fiction, poetry and fiction books. Doreen wrote and self-published over 50 books where she wrote about witchcraft, poverty, abuse: alcohol, drugs and power, citizens and refugees, youth, domestic workers, rejection and poetry.

She went through rejection by her mother, her late father, her late grandmother and late Aunt at home, in some churches and communities. Doreen suffered unemployment, poverty, loss of material possession, sickness and disease, miscarriages and rejection by her husband. She suffered racism in her home and communities. Her mother is Colored woman whose mother was White. She was rejected by some Vendas, Coloreds, Indians and foreign nationals. She was almost raped many times in the community and some churches. She was beaten as a child, deprived of food and clothing. She had to carry water from the well while still young.

She was brought up by her Aunt, Grandmother and mother. A life dominated by women for 4 decades. When Doreen got married these women fought her marriage through witchcraft. Doreen suffered in the hands of her Congolese mother-in-law and sister-in-law whom she invited from Democratic Republic of Congo.

Doreen was beaten up for going to church while she was a child but that did not stop her.

Doreen wrote some of her books while being unemployed and not owning a computer or laptop and no source of income. Some of the notebooks she found in garbage bins and also used old diaries which she asked from people to write her manuscripts.

She borrowed laptops, she cleaned internet café and was given time to type her books on computers of the internet café owners. These internet café owners were Congolese and Malawian. She also did some domestic work to earn some income and wrote books based on her experience. This she did in spite of being a qualified Human Resources Officer and Skills Development Facilitator. God has honored her hard work in that her books are available world-wide.

When she started schooling, her class was under a tree. They sat on stones and wrote on the ground using their fingers or pieces of sticks to write. On rainy days Doreen did not attend school. She walked bare feet to school and wore over-sized clothes and sometimes torn clothes. Children mocked Doreen of her oversized clothes. She did most of her studying on a tree as that was the only quiet place she could find.

She endured beatings by teachers, bullies at school and was beaten at home as well. God used a Missionary White Doctor, her Sunday school teacher and some of the school teachers to mold her life.

Doreen learned to speak English at age 16 at an Indian school. All her teachers were Indians and about 97% of students where Indians. She failed Accounting and chose to do Typing in the middle of the year. Doreen approached the school principal, (Indian) and asked him to change her Accounting subject to Typing. She did not know much English then. His response was that "my dear, it was never done in this school before". Her response was, Sir, let me be the first one. He approved her request. Little did she know she will use the typing skill to type her books many years to come.

She did all her subjects in lower grade because the teachers thought she was not intelligent enough to make it. Only two of her teachers encouraged her to achieve in life. Most of her teachers regarded her poverty, inability to speak English, her IQ as that that she could not even enter college doors. Her Accounting teacher (Indian) said to her "*Doreen, you are good for the streets*". He meant she should be a prostitute.

She studied at an Afrikaans/English college where 95% of students were Whites and 100% of lecturers were Whites. She learned dicta-typing and secretarial skills. She walked to and from college about 5km a day. Her White lecturers notice her determination and helped her.

She claims not to have achieved rather she glories God for enabling her to write life changing stories. God asked Abraham "*Is there anything too hard for the LORD?*" The answer is the same as it was then, NOTHING is too hard for our God.

She wrote most of her books with limited resources, seating on the floor, old bed, old couch, buckets, without a proper table. She had no anti-virus software and lost some of her manuscripts and had to retype them.

BOOKS BY DOREEN MAMPANI

Non fiction	Fiction	Poetry
Who Owns Your Soul?	Dolina: A Novel. Vol. 1	The Storeroom Gives Birth to a Story
Who Owns Your Soul? Revised Edition	Dolina: A Novel. Vol. 2	Tribulation Escorting Triumph
Who Owns Your Soul? Series. Vol. 1	Dolina: A Novel. Vol. 3	Author Without a Pen
Who Owns Your Soul? Series. Vol. 2		44 Liters of Tears
Who Owns Your Soul? Series Vol. 3		The Plague in the Fatherless Home
Who Owns Your Soul? Series. Vol. 4		Great Departure of Mortals
Who Owns Your Soul? Series. Vol. 5		Little Oil in My Lamp
Who Owns Your Soul? Series. Vol. 6		The Song, The Dance, The Table and the Dinning of Souls
Sin Tantalizers		Riding On The Back Of A Poor Man
The Reigning of the Refugee		Silencing The Laughter of Goliath
The Citizens Bow to the Refugees		Shacks Paving Way for Mansions
Log of Poverty in the Eye		Not Yet Time
Awakening of the Impoverished Prince		No Need to Die Early
Deceiving Voice of Poverty		Drops of Tears in the Desert
Trapped in the Underworld		44 Years and 4 Months
Dinning With Deception in the Shrine		Tears of a Domestic Worker
Deadly Diabolical Games		Heart of Stone in Dire Need of Heart of Flesh
Dethroning Poverty from the Golden Throne		Nobody Thinks About Me But I Must Think About Them
Uprooting the Bitter Roots of Abuse		Last Drink, Last Meal
Monster in Mama is Not Bigger than God		Tenacity Of A Maid
Monster in Mama is not Bigger		Youth Searching For A Role Model

than God. Revised Edition		
Venom of a Bitter Woman		*Past Shame, Present Pain, Future Gain.*
Venom of a Bitter Woman. Revised Edition.		*Souls In A Clay Pot*
Wages Of Laborers Cry Out		*Tormented by Tokoloshe Delivered by LORD Jesus Christ*
Exhilaration Of Buying Now And The Excruciating Pain Of Paying Later		*What Is The Color Of Souls? Poetry on Interracial Marriages*
Beyond Four Borders		*Women Without Wombs: Lamentations of the Childless*
Dethroned Deities		*Once the Outcast Colored People*
A Soul In A Bottle: Pain Of Domestic Violence		*Divorce the Rival of Marriage: Do not Hate the One who Hurt You*
Mama Lost The Charm		*My Once Depressed Soul*
Souls Amongst Lions: Battle In The Valley Of Death		*When The Owner Of Souls Comes*
Soulish Prayers Diabolical Prayers		*Beyond Death: Where LORD Jesus Christ The Son Of God Is The Sun*
Divorcing My Deceptive Refugee Husband		*My Trials, My Tribulations, My Triumphant Ascending To Heaven*
'Til Money Do Us Part: Marriage of Convenience To A Refugee		*Yesterday My Pain, Today My Poem, Tomorrow My Praise*
Lamentations for My Refugee X-Husband		*Once Betrayed, Twice Betrayed, But Never Dismayed*
Tokoloshe: Spirits are Forbidden to Marry Humans		*Love Does Not Go On Holiday*
Who's Womb Is It?		*If I Lived A 1000 Years*